MEASURE IT!

DISTANCE, AREA, AND VOLUME

Barbara A. Somervill

Heinemann
LIBRARY

Chicago, Illinois

www.heinemannraintree.com
Visit our website to find out more information about Heinemann-Raintree books.

To order:
☎ Phone 888-454-2279
💻 Visit www.heinemannraintree.com to browse our catalog and order online.

Edited by Megan Cotugno, Louise Galpine, and Abby Colich
Designed by Richard Parker
Original illustrations ©Darren Lingard, 2009
Picture research by Mica Brancic
Originated by Capstone Global Library, Ltd.
Printed and bound in China by CTPS

13 12 11 10
10 9 8 7 6 5 4 3 2 1

Library of Congress Cataloging-in-Publication Data

Somervill, Barbara A.
  Distance, area, and volume / Barbara A. Somervill.
    p. cm. -- (Measure it!)
  Includes bibliographical references and index.
  ISBN 978-1-4329-3763-8 (hc) -- ISBN 978-1-4329-3769-0 (pb) 1. Distances--Measurement--Juvenile literature. 2. Area measurement--Juvenile literature. 3. Volume (Cubic content)--Juvenile literature. I. Title.
  QC102.S66 2010
  516'.15--dc22
                      2009035191

Acknowledgments

The author and publishers are grateful to the following for permission to reproduce copyright material:

Alamy p. 7 (©Image Source Pink); Corbis p. 18 (TempSport/ ©Jerome Prevost); Getty Images p. 28 (Stone/GK Hart/Vikki Hart); iStockphoto pp. 12 (rest), 20 (©M. Eric Honeycutt), 23 (©Ufuk ZIVANA), 24 (©Graça Victoria), 25 (©Kriss Russell), 27 (©franklin lugenbeel); Photolibrary pp. 4 (Corbis), 16 (©Pixtal Imaes); Shutterstock pp. 5 (©Racheal Grazias), 11 (©Yulli), 13 (©Zoom Team), 15 (©Erwin Wodicka).

Cover photo of liquid being poured into a beaker reproduced with permission from Shutterstock (©Elemental Imaging).

We would like to thank John Pucek for his invaluable help in the preparation of this book.

Every effort has been made to contact copyright holders of any material reproduced in this book. Any omissions will be rectified in subsequent printings if notice is given to the publisher.

All the Internet addresses (URLs) given in this book were valid at the time of going to press. However, due to the dynamic nature of the Internet, some addresses may have changed, or sites may have changed or ceased to exist since publication. While the author and publisher regrets any inconvenience this may cause readers, no responsibility for any such changes can be accepted by either the author or the publisher.

Contents

Some words are printed in bold, **like this**. You can find out what they mean by looking in the glossary on page 30.

What Is Distance?

Within minutes of your birth, a nurse measured you to see how long you were. The average newborn baby measures 51 centimeters (20 inches) long. Do you know how long you were when you were born? Once you could stand up, your length became height. Doctors measure children to see if they are growing at a normal rate. At ten years old, the average child measures 142 centimeters (56 inches) tall. Are you taller or shorter than average?

Measuring children's growth is one way to see if children are healthy.

Length, height, and distance are all the same type of measurement. They measure the space between one point and another point on a straight line. Sometimes distance measurements must be accurate. The winning pole vault at a track and field meet was 5.9 meters (19.4 feet). We use an exact measure to determine the winner. Sometimes, an **estimate** of distance is close enough. The Earth is about 150 million kilometers (93 million miles) from the sun. We do not need to know this measurement to the exact meter.

Measuring distance in the past

Thousands of years ago, people did not have rulers or tape measures. They used body parts as measuring tools. The inch was the width of an adult thumb. A foot was measured as an adult foot. A yard measured from the tip of an adult's nose to the middle finger on an outstretched arm. Longer distances were measured by "pacing" a distance. A pace was the length of an adult man's long step. A field might have measured 80 paces by 110 paces.

Body part measuring was not accurate. Not all adults' arms, thumbs, and feet are the same length. Everyone's measurements were different. People needed something consistent. So they started using **barleycorns**. Three barleycorns laid end-to-end equaled one inch. This was fine for short distances, but it would take thousands of barleycorns and too much time to measure a mile.

This pole-vaulter jumped 5.9 meters to win.

EXPERIMENT!

Try an experiment at home. Choose six small items and put them on a table. Ask an adult to measure each using only hands, feet, or fingers. Record each measurement. Now repeat the measurements using your own hands, feet, and fingers. What did you find out?

The metric system

In the late 1700s, the French were using many different measurement units. In 1790 the National Assembly of France asked the Academy of Sciences to develop **standard** measurement units that were easy to use. The Academy created the International System of Units, which we call the metric system. The unit of distance called the meter was 1/10,000,000 of the distance from the North Pole to the **equator** along the **line of longitude** that passed through Dunkerque, France.

The meter gets its name from the Greek word *metron*, which means "measure." Today, most countries use millimeters, centimeters, meters, and kilometers to measure length. These units are all based on the meter, and all measures in the metric system are based on the number ten.

Meter Chart

Unit	Equals...
1 millimeter (mm)	0.001 meter (m)
1 centimeter (cm)	0.01 meter
1 kilometer (km)	1,000 meters

The metric system is practical for all distance measurements. Millimeters (mm) are perfect for measuring the **diameter** of wire. We measure the length of a newborn baby in centimeters (cm). The length of a building is measured in meters (m). Long distances, like the length from one town to another, are measured in kilometers (km). Metric measurements are easy to use, for short or long distance measurements.

The U.S. customary system

In the United States, people use the imperial system, also called the U.S. customary system of measurements. This includes inches, feet, yards, and miles. The measurement of a foot comes from the Romans who decided that a foot should be 12 inches. Every nation the Romans conquered—including most of Europe and the Middle East—used a 12-inch foot as a standard measure.

Common U.S. Distance Units

Unit	Equals...
1 foot (ft.)	12 inches (in.)
1 yard (yd.)	3 ft.
1 mile (mi.)	1,760 yd. or 5,280 ft.

Converting Metric to Imperial and Imperial to Metric

Metric Unit	Imperial Equivalent	Imperial Unit	Metric Equivalent
1 millimeter (mm)	0.0394 inches (in.)	1 inch	2.54 cm
1 centimeter (cm)	0.393 inches (in.)	1 foot	30.48 cm
1 meter (m)	1.093 yards (yd.)	1 yard	0.914 m
1 kilometer (km)	0.621 miles (mi.)	1 mile	1.609 km

A measuring tape is a common way to measure short distances.

Did You Know?
Need to measure a short distance but don't have a ruler? Use a dollar bill. United States dollars are about six inches long. Two dollars laid end-to-end are approximately one foot.

Tools for measuring distance

The tools we use to measure distance depend on the size of the distance. A ruler can measure millimeters and centimeters or inches and feet. A meter stick or a yardstick is fine for the height of a person, but you need a long tape measure for the length of a building. In your car, an **odometer** measures the miles or kilometers you travel.

Measuring very long distances or tall heights can be difficult. Sometimes people use **global positioning systems (GPS)** to measure long distances. GPS calculates distance using computer technology.

You Do the Math

Max needs to go from Elmdale to Newton. Using a metric ruler, measure the distance from Elmdale to Newton on the map. The scale of this map is 1 centimeter equals 20 kilometers. How far does Max need to travel if he takes the most direct route?

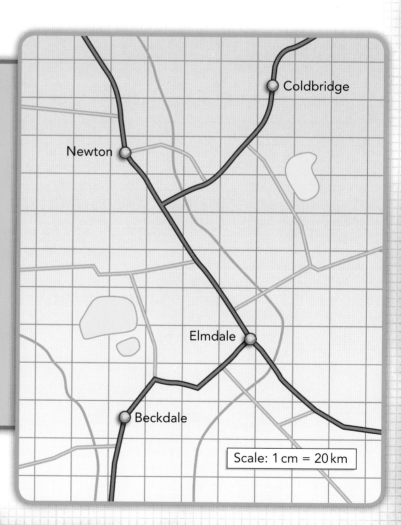

Newton

Coldbridge

Elmdale

Beckdale

Scale: 1 cm = 20 km

You Do the Math

You can find the height of tall trees and buildings using geometry and **ratios**. The distance from the base point to the woman is 5 meters (A). The distance from the base point to the tree is 50 meters (B). From the base point, the top of the woman's head lines up with the top of the tree. The diagram shows two **right triangles**. The ratio of the woman's height to distance A is the same as the ratio of the tree's height to distance B.

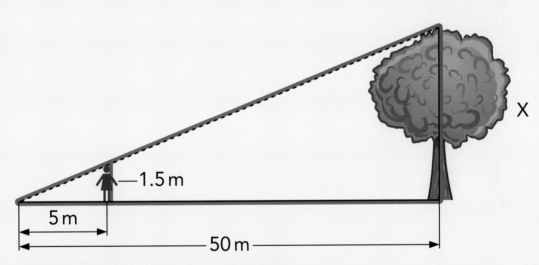

1.5 m is to 5 m as X m is to 50 m.
50 m is 10 times longer than 5 m.
Multiply 1.5 m × 10 to find that the tree is 15 m tall.

What Is a Great Circle?

We're taking a trip from San Francisco, California, to London, England. The airline company wants to follow the shortest route to save jet fuel. Of course, they must consider air traffic and storms, but the fastest route around the Earth is along a **great circle**.

The shortest distance around the Earth is along a great circle.

If you look at a map of the world, you can draw a line from San Francisco to London. The route seems to be a good one, but there is a problem. The Earth is not flat like the map. It is more like a **sphere**. We should plan a route based on the shape of the Earth, not on a flat map.

A great circle is a circle that runs along the surface of a sphere. If a great circle passed through the Earth, it would cut the Earth exactly in half. The line it drew would pass through Earth's exact center. The **equator** is a great circle. **Lines of longitude** are also great circles.

Finding great circles

Several hundred years ago, ship navigators wanted to find fast routes to deliver their cargo to port. The ships traveled the shortest, quickest routes to save time and money. The ships traveled along great circles as much as possible.

Look at a globe. Using your finger, draw a great circle from San Francisco to London. You will find that the shortest route takes you over the North Pole. Continue drawing your great circle. Your great circle that connects San Francisco to London continues on to Rome, Italy, and other places in the world. Traveling the shortest distance saves time, money, and fuel.

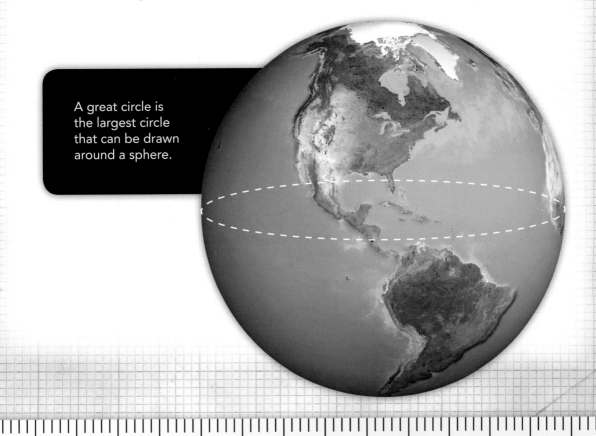

A great circle is the largest circle that can be drawn around a sphere.

What Is Area?

You can measure the length or height of your desk using a ruler. You can also measure the amount of space taken up the surface of your desk. This is called area. All the space inside a circle is a circle's area. The land or site on which a building stands is the area of the land. Area can be any size or shape. The head of a pin, a farm, and a continent all have area. Area is measured using distance measurements. Length and width are distance measurements. The **radius** and **diameter** of a circle are also distance measurements.

Using area

A golf course's fairways and greens must be mowed every day. The golf course covers 16 hectares (40 acres) of land. The course manager figures that one worker can mow 2 hectares (5 acres) a day. Based on the total area of the course, he needs to hire eight workers for mowing. The manager uses area to develop a work schedule.

Oxen were once used to measure area, but the measurements were not all consistent.

As far back as ancient China, Egypt, and Mesopotamia, land was granted, bought, sold, and farmed according to area. People paid taxes based on the area of land that they owned.

Seed measure always refers to grain crops, never fruit or vegetables.

Area and the metric system

Many countries measure area using the metric system. The metric system uses hectares to measure farmland. One hectare equals 100 meters by 100 meters. The abbreviation for hectares is ha. The area of a city is usually measured in square kilometers, which is written as km^2. For example, Rome, Italy, covers 1,285.3 km^2.

The area of a house or school is measured in square meters. A square meter is one meter by one meter, which is written as m^2. The area of small surfaces, such as tile, is measured in square centimeters. A square centimeter is one centimeter by one centimeter and is written cm^2.

Area and the U.S. customary system

In the U.S. customary system, square inches (sq. in.), square feet (sq. ft.), square yards (sq. yd.), and square miles (sq. mi.) are used to measure area. People use the most convenient units for what they are measuring. For example, a picture might take up 140 sq. in. of wall space. Carpeting a room might require 120 sq. ft. of carpet. A town might stretch 14 sq. mi. of land.

Conversion Chart

Units for Measuring Area	Multiply by...	To get...
1 acre (ac.)	0.405	0.405 hectares
1 hectare (ha)	2.471	2.471 acres
1 square mile (sq. mi.)	2.6	2.6 square kilometers
1 square kilometer (km^2)	0.386	0.386 square miles
1 square yard (sq. yd.)	0.84	0.84 square meters
1 square meter (m^2)	1.2	1.2 square yards

Knowing surface area is very useful. In the home, measure the area of wall space to plan for wallpaper or paint, or the area of floor space for carpeting. Measure the area of a yard to figure out how much grass seed is needed. We buy land for homes or farming by area.

How do you know how much paint to buy? You figure out the area of wall space that needs to be covered!

You Do the Math

A farm owner in Texas donates land to the county for a park. The old **deed** says the land covers 76 sq. mi. The county officials want to know how many km² of land they have to work with. How many km² equals 76 sq. mi.? Use the chart on the left to find out.

What Units Are Used When Measuring Area?

A clothing company makes hundreds of pairs of jeans every day. The company manager needs to order enough fabric to make the jeans. How does she know how much fabric to order? First she arranges the pattern for the jeans on fabric, being careful not to waste any fabric. The manager finds that one pair of jeans requires 1.3 m^2 of fabric. One hundred pairs of jeans require 130 m^2 of cloth.

To make a hundred pairs of jeans, manufacturers carefully figure out the area of the fabric they need.

Common area measurement units include metric and imperial units. Metric area measures are all based on the square meter. The most common units used are square centimeters, square meters, square kilometers, and hectares.

Relationship of Metric Units to the Meter

Metric Area Unit	Relationship to the meter
square centimeter (cm^2)	.01 meter x .01 meter ($0.0001\ m^2$)
square meter (m^2)	1 meter x 1 meter ($1\ m^2$)
hectare (ha)	100 meters x 100 meters ($10,000\ m^2$)
square kilometer (km^2)	1,000 meters x 1,000 meters ($1,000,000\ m^2$)

The United States uses imperial units or U.S. customary units for measuring area. The most common units are square inches, square feet, square yards, square miles, and acres. The chart shows the relationship between these measurement units.

U.S. Area Measurement Units

Unit	Equals...
1 square foot (sq. ft.)	144 square inches (sq. in.)
1 square yard (sq. yd.)	9 square feet (sq. ft.)
1 acre (ac.)	4,840 square yards (sq. yd.)
1 square mile (sq. mi.)	640 acres (ac.)

Did You Know?
Area measurement is expressed in square units, such as square meters or square kilometers. In metric units, the symbol that means square is a small 2 raised above the abbreviation of the unit. It looks like this: $5\ m^2$ or $5\ km^2$.

A **standard** soccer field is rectangular. It can measure 46 to 92 m (150 to 300 ft.) wide by 92 to 119 m (300 to 390 ft.) long. The largest field (92 x 119 m) takes up more than twice as much area as the smaller field (46 x 92 m).

To measure area, we use formulas based on common shapes. The four basic shapes for measuring area are squares, rectangles, triangles, and circles. To find area, use the math formula for each shape. Squares and rectangles are easy. Multiply the length by the width. Triangles use the same idea, but they have a different formula. For the area of a triangle, use the formula area equals ½ of the base (the bottom of the triangle) multiplied by the height.

Here is an example: A triangle measures 4 cm along the base. The height of the triangle is the distance from the base to the highest part of the triangle. If the height of the triangle is 6 cm, then the area of the triangle is ½ of 4 cm times 6 cm, which equals 12 cm^2.

Figuring out the areas of countries, states, or counties is a bit harder. Few large land areas have straight borders. Most borders follow rivers, coastlines, or major land features. The way to figure out the area of any uneven shape is the same for a small backyard as it is for a country. Break the area into common shapes: squares, rectangles, circles or parts of circles, and triangles. Figure out the area of each smaller shape and add the area of all the shapes together.

Tools for measuring

We use many of the same tools to measure area as we use to measure distance. Small areas can be measured with a ruler, measuring tape, or measuring stick. Larger areas can be measured using a **distance wheel**. The person measuring the land pushes the distance wheel along the outside border of the land being measured. Today's distance wheels have computers attached and can quickly figure out the area of land.

You Do the Math

Frank wants to plant grass in his yard, but the yard is an odd shape. One bag of grass seed covers 100 m². Figure out the area of Frank's yard and decide if he has enough grass seed.

HINT: Divide the shape into 1 rectangle and 2 **right triangles**. Figure out the area of each shape and add the areas together.

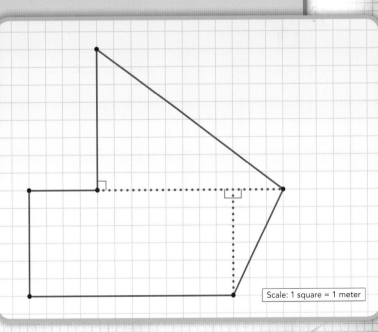

Scale: 1 square = 1 meter

Does Our Furniture Fit?

When you are moving from one home to another or one room to another, there is always one question that needs answering: How will the furniture fit into the room? One way to find the answer is to make a floor plan.

Figure out the length of each wall and the total area of the floor.

Here is what you will need to make your floor plan: 2 pieces of graph paper, a tape measure or yardstick, a pencil, scissors, glue, and a compass, if you have any round furniture. Ready? Then, let's begin. Start by measuring the length of each wall in the new room. Write down the measurements and transfer the information onto the graph paper. Allow one square for every foot. For a wall that measures 12 feet long, draw a line 12 squares long. When you have all the walls drawn on your plan, measure and mark doorways and closets on your floor plan.

Next, measure each piece of furniture going in the room. Draw the shape of each furniture piece on your other sheet of graph paper, using the same scale as your floor plan. One square equals one foot. Label each furniture piece. Cut the shapes out. Next, place the furniture shapes on your floor plan. Move them around until they fit where you want them to go. Be sure to leave room to open your door. When the plan is finished, glue the furniture shapes onto the plan. You can use the floor plan as a guide when arranging your furniture.

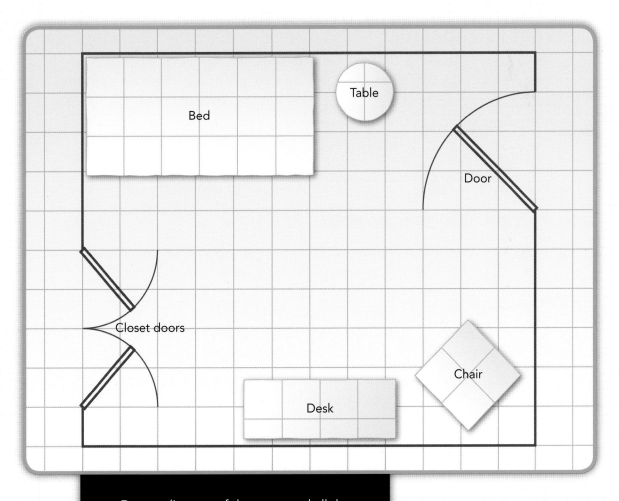

Draw a diagram of the room and all the furniture to scale on graph paper. Cut out the furniture pieces and place them in the room's space.

What Is Volume?

Volume and capacity are two ways to measure the size of three-dimensional objects. Volume refers to how much space an object takes up. To find volume or capacity, we use distance measurements. A plastic container measures 10 centimeters long, 5 centimeters wide, and 20 centimeters high. To find the volume of the container, multiply the three measurements together. The volume of the container is 1,000 cubic centimeters (cm³). Volume can also mean the amount a container holds, such as a liter, a gallon, or a teaspoon.

What is capacity?

Capacity is slightly different than volume. Capacity measures the amount an object holds. Every day, drivers fill up their cars with fuel. The amount of fuel each fuel tank holds is the tank's capacity. The capacity of the average small car's fuel tank is about 49 liters (13 gallons).

You Do the Math

Chris offered to make punch for a class party. His recipe only serves 8 people, but there are 24 in his class, including his teacher. Here are the ingredients from the recipe he plans to use:

250 ml cranberry juice   175 ml apple juice
325 ml ginger ale   125 ml raspberry sherbet

To make enough punch for the class, Chris must multiply the volume of each ingredient by 3. How much of each ingredient does he need?

Eggs are ellipsoid or ovoid shapes. Every egg is slightly different in size, so each has a slightly different volume.

Solid shapes have volume. The most common solid shapes are cones, cylinders, cubes, rectangular solids, and **spheres**. There are also ellipsoids shaped like eggs, tetrahedrons shaped like pyramids, and several other solid shapes. These solids have three dimensions. Depending on the shape, most solids have length, width, and height. Spheres are "solid circles," and their measurements depend on the **radius** of the circle and **pi (π)**, which equals approximately 3.142. Pi is a number that is used when measuring circles. This includes solid round shapes, such as spheres, egg shapes, cones, or cylinders.

Using capacity and volume

Capacity measures how much a container holds when it is filled to the top. It is the ability of a container to hold, receive, or absorb substances. A glass holds liquid. Soil holds rainwater, and a sponge absorbs liquid. Glasses, soil, and sponges have capacity.

Volume is used every day in cooking, packaging, and shipping. Businesses want to use the best shape and size when packaging a product. They must label most food products according to either volume or weight. Shipping across a city or across an ocean also uses volume. Shippers need to figure out how much of their product will fit into a shipping container.

When baking, we usually measure liquid ingredients by volume. This container measures cups, ounces, liters, and milliliters.

What Units Are Used When Measuring Volume?

If a hot air balloon is filled with air, why does it rise? The answer is that a volume of hot air weighs less than the same volume of cold air. One cubic meter (35 cubic feet) of air heated to 38°C (100°F) weighs about 250 grams (9 ounces) less than the same volume of cold air. Each cubic meter of heated air lifts 250 grams (9 ounces) of weight, which explains why hot air balloons are so big. A balloon needs a huge volume of hot air to lift the balloon, basket, and riders.

If there is not a large enough volume of heated air in a hot air balloon, the balloon will not fly.

In the metric system, we measure volume by cubic centimeters (cm³) and cubic meters (m³). Car engines are measured in cubic centimeters. Garden mulch, topsoil, and concrete are measured in cubic meters. **Capacity** is measured in milliliters (ml) and liters (l). When baking, vanilla and milk are measured in milliliters. The capacity of a large soda bottle is 2 liters.

In your home, you use volume and capacity measurements all the time. You have containers in the kitchen for storing flour, sugar, coffee, and tea. You have baking dishes, pots, and pans that hold different amounts of food for cooking.

In the United States, people use U.S. customary measurement units for measuring volume and capacity. Volume is measured is cubic inches (cu. in.), cubic feet (cu. ft.), and cubic yards (cu. yd.). You might measure a box of candy in cubic inches, a refrigerator in cubic feet, and cement in cubic yards. Common capacity measurements are pints, quarts, and gallons. You might buy a pint of cream, a quart of oil for the car, and a gallon of gasoline.

Metric to U.S. Customary Measures Conversion Chart

Metric to U.S. Customary	U.S. Customary to Metric
10 ml = 2 teaspoons	1 teaspoon = 5 ml
10 ml = 2/3 tablespoon	1 tablespoon = 15 ml
500 ml = 2.1 cups	1 cup = 237 ml
1 l = 2.1 pints	1 pint = 0.47 l
1 l = 1.01 quarts	1 quart = 0.9 l
1 l = 0.26 gallon	1 gallon = 3.8 l

Cooks and bakers often measure ingredients in special containers. These include teaspoons (tsp), tablespoons (tbsp), and cups. These tools measure salt, spices, flour, sugar, and other ingredients.

Did You Know?
Volume measurement is expressed in cubic units, such as cubic meters or cubic centimeters. In the metric system, the symbol that means cubic is a small 3 raised above the abbreviation of the units. It looks like this: 5 m^3 or 5 cm^3.

Volume: Metric to U.S. Customary Measures Conversion Chart

Metric to U.S. Customary	U.S. Customary to Metric
10 cm³ = 0.6 cu. in.	1 cu. in. = 16.4 cm³
1 m³ = 35 cu. ft.	1 cu. ft. = 0.03 m³
1 m³ = 1.3 cu. yd.	1 cu. yd. = 0.76 m³

To measure the volume of a solid shape, you need a ruler or a measuring tape. There are formulas for figuring out the volume of each shape. The volume of a cube or rectangular solid is the easiest to measure. Measure length, width, and height, and then multiply the measurements together. You measure a brick to see what the volume is. Multiply the length (20 cm) times the width (7 cm) to get 140. Next, multiply 140 times the height (8 cm) to get 1,120 cm³. That formula is easy.

This block is a cube. It measures the same distance on all sides. Find the volume of this cube by multiplying 5 cm x 5 cm x 5 cm. The volume is 125 cm³.

You Do the Math

Melissa's grandmother sent her an aquarium for her birthday. The tank holds 6 gallons of water. How many liters of water does the aquarium hold? HINT: Use the conversion chart on page 26 to figure out how many liters are in 1 gallon.

Answers to You Do the Math

What Is Distance? (page 8)

Use a ruler with centimeters to measure the distance on the map. The distance from Elmdale to Newton is 6 cm. The map scale is 1 cm = 20 km. Max must travel 6 multiplied by 20 km, which equals 120 km.

What Is Area? (page 15)

1 sq. mi. = 2.6 km^2

76 sq. mi. x 2.6 = 197.6 km^2

What Units Are Used When Measuring Area? (page 19)

To find the area of the rectangle, multiply 12 by 6, which equals 72 m^2.

To find the area of the top triangle, multiply 8 by 11, which equals 88. Take ½ of 88, which is 44 m^2.

To find the area of the rectangle to the right, multiply 6 by 3 to get 18. Take ½ of 18 to get 9 m^2.

Add the areas together: 44 + 72 + 9 = 125 m^2.

Frank only has grass seed for 100 m^2, so he needs to buy more.

What Is Volume? (page 22)

Chris multiplies each ingredient by 3 to get the amount needed:

250 ml x 3 = 750 ml cranberry juice

175 ml x 3 = 525 ml apple juice

325 ml x 3 = 975 ml ginger ale

125 ml x 3 = 375 ml raspberry sherbet

What Units Are Used When Measuring Volume? (page 28)

1 gallon = 3.8 liters

Multiply 6 gallons by 3.8 to equal 22.8 liters of water.

Glossary

barleycorn a grain of barley once used for measuring

capacity amount an object can hold, receive, or absorb

deed document saying a person owns something

diameter line through the center of a circle that measures the distance across the circle

dimension extension in a direction, such as a line

distance wheel tool consisting of a wheel, push rod, and meter that is used to measure distances of land

equator imaginary line around the center of the Earth

estimate approximate judgment of size

global positioning system (GPS) tool used for measuring distance

great circle a circle on the surface of a sphere

line of longitude imaginary line drawn from one of the Earth's poles to the other

odometer instrument for measuring distance traveled by a wheeled vehicle

pi (π) standard mathematical unit in measuring circles, spheres, and other rounded shapes, equals approximately 3.142

radius straight line from the center point to the outside of a circle or sphere

ratio a comparison of one number to another, particularly as to how many times the first number contains the second

right triangle a triangle in which one of the corners is a right angle

sphere round, solid shape

standard something considered the authority of a common size

volume the amount of space taken up by a three-dimensional object

Find Out More

Books

Levy, Janey. *The Great Pyramid of Giza: Measuring Length, Area, Volume, and Angles*. New York: Rosen, 2005.

Sullivan, Navin. *Measure Up! Area, Distance and Volume*. Tarrytown, N.Y.: Benchmark, 2006.

Trumbauer, Lisa. *What Is Volume?* Danbury, Conn.: Children's Press, 2006.

Woodford, Chris. *How Do We Measure? Volume*. Farmington Hills, Mich.: Blackbirch Press, 2005.

Websites

Math Playground
http://www.mathplayground.com/area_perimeter.html
Find the area and perimeter of rectangles.

Measuring area with maps
http://www.labnol.org/internet/tools/measure-area-home-football-stadium-with-google-maps/3373/
Measure the area of your home or a football field.

The U.S. Customary System
http://www.myschoolhouse.com/courses/0/1/18.asp
Complete some fun conversion problems on this website.

Index